Escape From The Comics

Written by N. M. Atode
Illustrated by Graeme Tavendale

Contents	Page
Chapter 1. *The idea*	4
Chapter 2. *Dynamo Man is created*	7
Chapter 3. *The action starts*	11
Chapter 4. *Famous at last!*	15
Chapter 5. *The plan*	20
Chapter 6. *Escape!*	26
Verse	32

Rigby

Escape From The Comics

With these characters ...

Dynamo Man

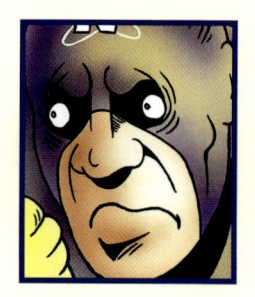

Nematode

Jeff

"BOOM

Setting the scene . . .

Ever wondered what it would be like to be a superhero? Well, you're about to find out from one of the most clever superheroes around.

Dynamo Man is the creation of Jeff, an illustrator, and together they become famous. But all is not well in the world of the superhero, and Dynamo Man is about to face the greatest challenge of his career. He can outsmart most of the evil characters in the comics—but will he be clever enough to outsmart the person who created him? He needs to come up with a plan. And for his plan to work, Dynamo Man needs to make a deal with his worst enemy— the evil Nematode!

BASH BIFF!"

Chapter 1.

I'm running! I'm hiding! I've escaped, and they're searching everywhere for me.

Who am I? How did I escape? To find out, you need to know the real story. My life story . . .

It all started late one Sunday night. Jeff, my creator, was bored and doodling on a piece of white paper when he had an idea. Well, he *thought* he had an idea.

Actually, I'd been in his mind for ages, just waiting for the right moment to escape. Poor old Jeff—he really wasn't that clever. It was *I* who made him a really famous illustrator.

But I'm telling you too much too soon. Let me tell you the story as it happened.

Jeff had been working as an illustrator of children's books—nice, ordinary children's books, in which everyone lived happily ever after. It was good work. But he was getting bored.

I had been wandering around in his mind, just waiting for the right time to introduce myself. I'd had a long time to wait, so I'd had plenty of time to make myself perfect. I looked *very* cool and *very* exciting!

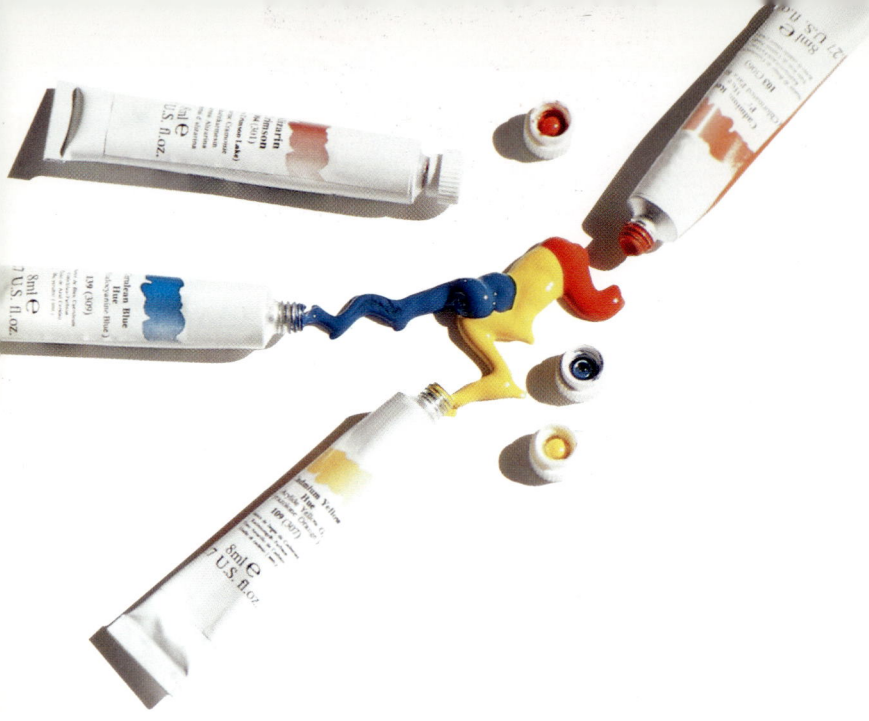

One weekend, Jeff had been working late on another ordinary children's book with pretty pictures and boring characters. I decided that enough was enough! It was time to escape from his mind and get *rrrr*-eal! I didn't want to watch any more pretty, boring illustrations being drawn in front of me. There are only so many flowers, puppies, and cute kids that I, a cool superhero, can take!

Chapter 2.

Inside Jeff's mind, I started making some noise. I started jumping up and down. I was really trying hard to get noticed. Now, I knew that Jeff was slow, but not *that* slow! It took hours before he finally put down his watercolor paints and picked up the black marker.

That's good, I said to myself. We're making progress here. Now just do as I tell you, Jeff, and you'll have the best-looking superhero character you've ever seen!

Now, I'm very easy to illustrate, aren't I? A few lines here, some curves there, and there I am. But, as I told you, Jeff is not clever. He was making me angry because he kept making mistakes, crossing out lines, redrawing them, and then drawing them too long.

Once, he became so annoyed he was going to screw up the piece of paper and go back to the children's book!

"No, DON'T DO IT!" I yelled. Wow, that was close.

A few more drafts, and there I was. Me. On the paper, large as life. The new comic book superhero: Dynamo Man!

Chapter 3.

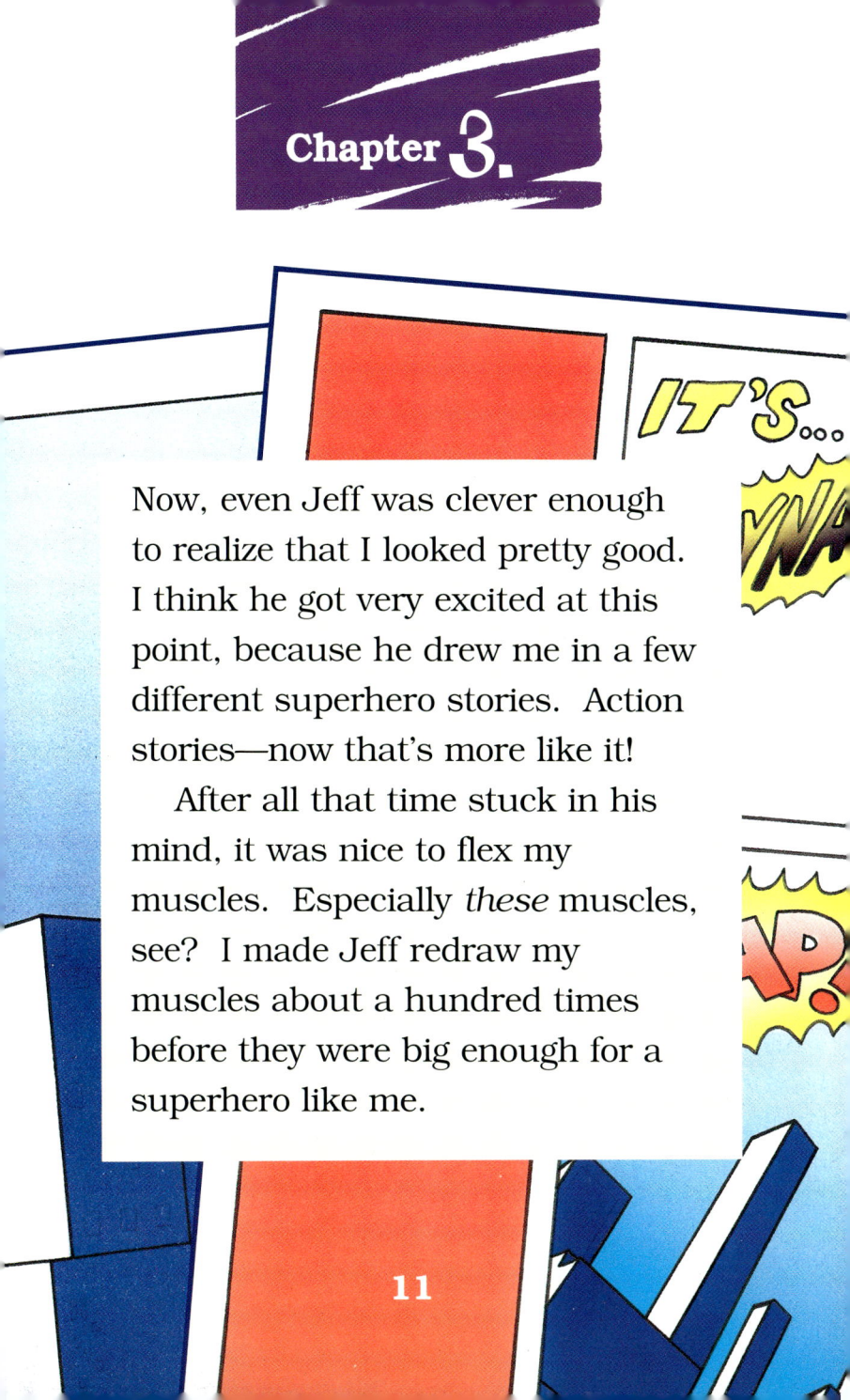

Now, even Jeff was clever enough to realize that I looked pretty good. I think he got very excited at this point, because he drew me in a few different superhero stories. Action stories—now that's more like it!

After all that time stuck in his mind, it was nice to flex my muscles. Especially *these* muscles, see? I made Jeff redraw my muscles about a hundred times before they were big enough for a superhero like me.

Pretty soon, we were working well together. I was telling Jeff what a great partnership we'd make. With his black marker pen and my instructions, I'd be the most successful comic superhero character in the world!

Don't let anyone tell you it's an easy job being a comic superhero. Just as soon as Jeff created me, along came some evil guy making trouble wherever he went. Usually, it was a mean character named Nematode, whom I had to fight with. But he's a pushover, really. He's never won a battle yet. Good old Dynamo Man to the rescue, saving the world from evil!

I could sure do with a hamburger now and again, and a nice chocolate milkshake. But the dumbo with the pen never remembers to illustrate any food or drinks for me.

Oh, yes. It's hungry, thirsty work protecting the world from bad guys!

Chapter 4.

So there we were. Jeff, Dynamo Man, and Nematode were now famous. All the kids loved us! We were selling thousands of comics every week as kids raced to the newsstand to buy each new issue.

We were having a great time as we BOOM BASH BIFFED our way through pages of action-packed superhero adventures. Jeff was having so much fun that he gave up on the wishy-washy children's books. Now he focused on action-packed adventures.

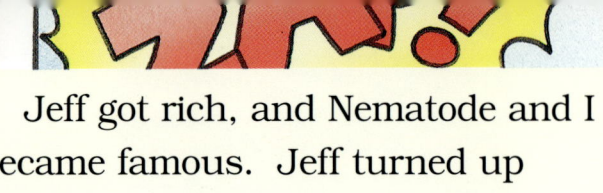

Jeff got rich, and Nematode and I became famous. Jeff turned up wherever I went—movie premieres, costume parties, parades. People even started talking about making a movie about me. I didn't think that they'd be able to find a human being handsome enough to play me. Little did I know, that was the least of my problems, because Jeff was about to prove what a dumbo he really was!

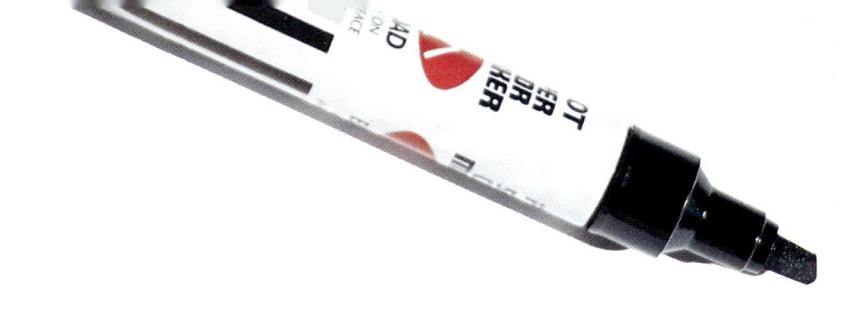

Right at the height of our popularity, the idiot dropped a bombshell. There I was, waiting for Jeff to illustrate another superhero action story when I overheard him on the phone.

"I'm going to get rid of him," he said. "Yes, I know he's famous, but I'm getting bored again."

Hey, wait a minute! Surely you're talking about Nematode? Not *me!* Just *who* is in charge here, Jeff?

I listen in and get the whole picture. It seemed as if the idiot was getting bored with drawing *me*.

Can you believe it? Bored! With Dynamo Man? Well, I had news for him, Mr. Illustrator. Dynamo Man is not someone you can just get rid of with an eraser. You forget . . . I *made* you famous. I *know* how to outsmart you!

Chapter 5.

So, in between the usual week's BOOM BASH BIFF comic stories with Nematode, I started working on my plan. It was crazy, I admit it, but it was the only way out of there. I didn't need this dumbo Jeff guy anymore! I was going out on my own. I was going to escape from the comics. I got into them. I could get out of them.

While Jeff left to sharpen his pencil, I had a quiet talk with Nematode. After weeks and weeks of getting knocked down and kicked around by me, he was ready to listen to my escape plan.

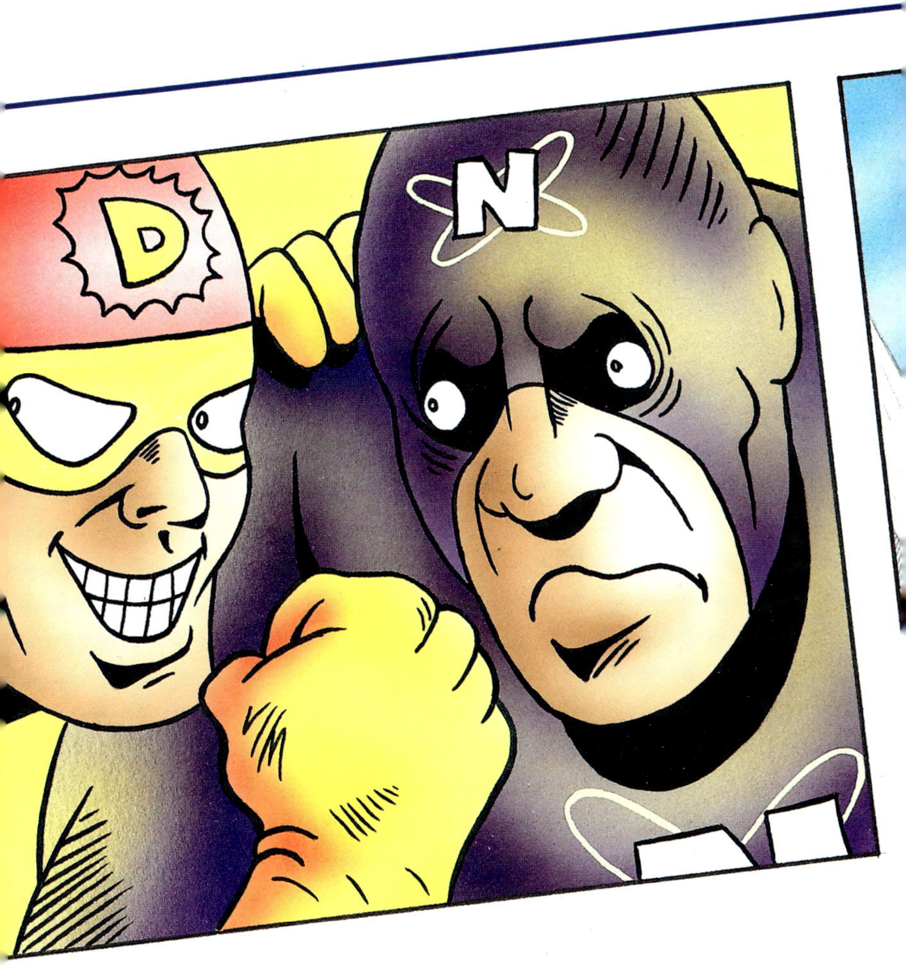

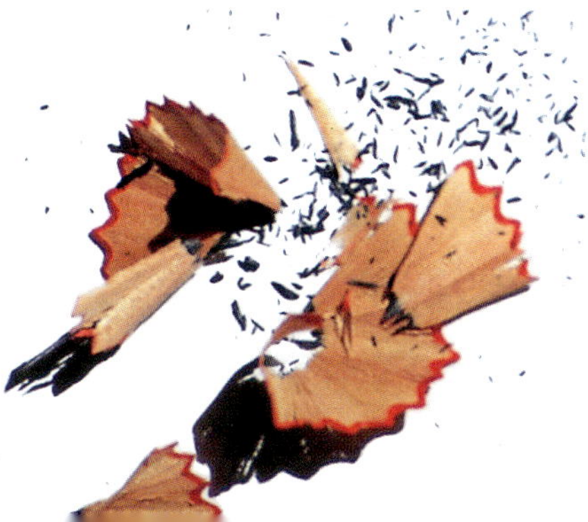

"You and me, my *good* friend, have got better places to go," I said in my most friendly voice.

Nematode looked surprised. "Whatever you say, Dynamo Man," he said.

I like a bad guy who knows I'm the boss.

"When Jeff gets back, you know we're going to have to do the BOOM BASH BIFF action stuff," I said. Nematode nodded and rubbed his jaw.

"Only this time," I said, "I'm going to fake it." Nematode frowned, and looked puzzled.

"And when Jeff goes to make his next cup of coffee, you're going to help me up to the edge of the picture. I'm going to make a run for it!"

Nematode looked at me as if I was crazy. But when I flexed my muscles, he was convinced that he should do exactly what I said.

"OK," he said. "But I'm coming too."

Well, that seemed fair enough. I mean, how much harm can the guy really do? He only wanted to rule the world.

Jeff finally returned and started drawing the day's action adventure. But this time, we were ready for him. I took a swing at Nematode, and he dropped to the floor as if he'd been acting all his life. The guy should get an acting award! Then, as Jeff left to make another cup of coffee, we put our escape plan into action.

Chapter 6.

Nematode dusted himself off and helped me up to the corner of the picture frame. I clambered up and gave him a hand up. Hey, for a couple of comic characters and mortal enemies, we were working well together.

We had to move quickly now. Nematode kept an eye out for Jeff while I surveyed the edge of the page. It looked safe to me, so I made a dash for it. Nematode was right behind me. All we had to do was make it to the fold in the middle of the page. Then we slipped under the paper and slipped right out of sight.

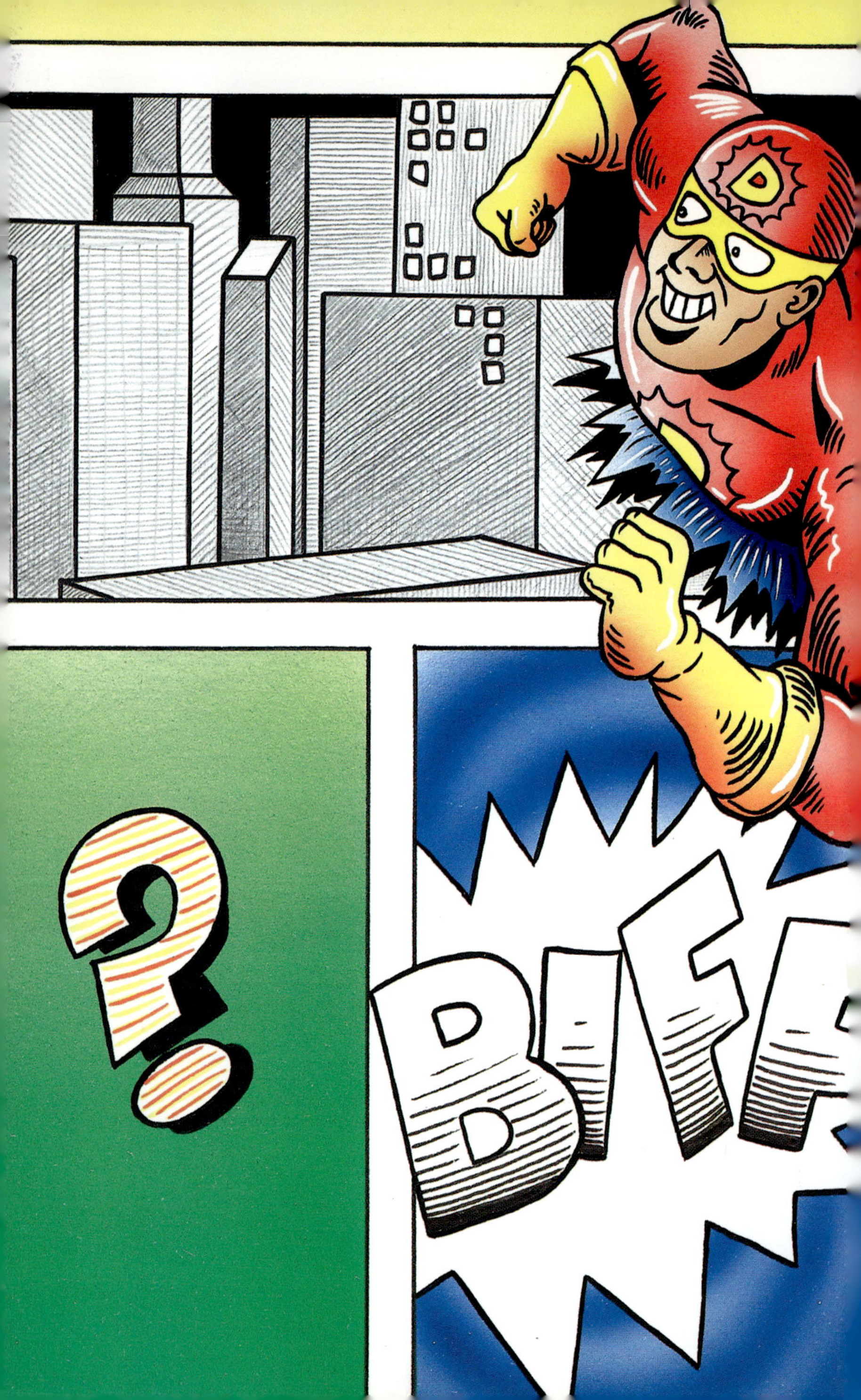
?
BIF

BOP!

Well, I guess by now you've figured out that the escape plan worked perfectly. We made it off the paper, down the desk, along the floor, and slipped out through the kitchen. Jeff was still there, stirring his coffee, by the time we made it to the hallway.

I turned to Nematode and we gave each other the superhero handshake. He turned and took off toward the elevator. That was the last I saw of him.

So, now I'm a superhero on the run. It's not so bad. Maybe I'll start a superhero theme park. Or maybe I'll open a superhero restaurant. Whatever I end up doing, I'll be successful. As you know, I can do *anything*, if I try hard enough!

As for Nematode, he's bored with being an evil character. He just wants a quiet life. He says he'll write children's books. I hope he makes it.

I told him that a story about our escape might make a good book. I wonder if he'll ever do it.

"BOOM BASH BIFF!"

Even heroes can get the chop
So they say, it's tough at the top
Comics are where it's at
Apparently Jeff is bored with that
Perhaps it's time to start anew
Exit the page, before I'm through!